T0065578

POETRY

Pacemaker

BY

PAULETTE LEWIS

authorHOUSE®

AuthorHouse™
1663 Liberty Drive
Bloomington, IN 47403
www.authorhouse.com
Phone: 1 (800) 839-8640

Published by AuthorHouse 09/21/2016

ISBN: 978-1-5246-4033-0 (sc)
ISBN: 978-1-5246-4032-3 (e)

Contents

Find True Peace

The beauty within will withstand
Every storm.
The strength of your faith will
Carry you through.
Your smile will get brighter
Radiating from the abundance of
Love around you.
Finding true peace, is a stem from
Your soul.
Be calm in your most difficult times
Monitor your heart rate
Breathe easy.
True peace within, your heart.

Balance Your Life

Every time you step out into
This wicked world. Find balance
Every time you break bread
Find balance within yourself.
Every time you find another true
Friend, be grateful.
Balance your life, don't use up all
Energy. Save some for new adventures
Stay focus when everyone is at your
Beck and call.
Enjoy a balance diet blanket, wrap in
A safety net for comfort.

Pacemaker

You might need a pacemaker someday
Embrace this energy with a word of
Thought. The butterflies will forever
Be the center of a surgery.
But our creator is still in charge.
Embrace life to the highest capacity
Love and enjoy daily.
Slow heartbeat, very slow heart rate
Deep breathing,a relaxed mind in everything
Your choice, your personal choice to keep
I am with you always. A forever gift.

Forever Loved

Your gifts will be shared
Your love will be remembered
By all.
Your kindness will be a shelter
A college and foundation amongst
Your people.
Forever loved by the one who jump start
Your heart.
Gone for so long, yet will never be forgotten.

When You Lost A Friend

A friend until the end
A friend in difficult times
A friend in time of despair
A friend in the beginning of
Everything wonderful.
Surrounded by pure and genuine
Love, shining through the window
From my soul to yours.
Rest peacefully my friend.
Forever bonded with one true friend.
Now my guardian angel.

I Will Forever Be Grateful

Forever my gratitude tree will remember
Your face.
Forever your kindness lives closer to my
Heart.
Forever the aspect of one's mind will capture
That gratitude chart.
Give more than you receive, the payback and
Reward is in heaven.
Pray and wash away all your sins, gifted is the
Soul of mankind.
I will forever be grateful. For everything.
Everyone is an open book, read and comprehend
True gratitude. Humble is true grace.

Bright House

Plug in my favorite chanel
Show me my favorite show
Play my favorite song
Then read me a poem.
Open the windows to let the sun
In. Fresh breeze to glide away this
Feelings.
Give me the chill pill for a comfort
Zone. Assist only in your scope.
Send in the birds to sing me a melody
Just for a moment, let my doggy sit in
Space. This is a bright house filled with
Everything beautiful. Even the sound of
Hospice fears me not.
Time well spent on earth, beautiful people
Not enough to go around.
Be bless, we will meet again in heaven.

Brave And Bold

The worse is yet to come
Gear up and enjoy your life now.
Disappoint not in the things that
You have done.
Rejoice in the Lord instead.
Your challenge in life is fully
Understood by one.
He's the mentor for your surgery
He know everything ahead of time.
Worry not, the keeper of your
Pacemaker is on daily duty
Be not afraid, be bold and brave.

This Summer

Make this your best summer
Enjoy every moment with a smile
Share your love with others.
Celebrate under the palm tree
Spend this quiet moment with me.
Give my heart a boost, i will then
Pass it over to see your truth.
Mayday is on the back burner
Every moment is well spent.
My faith family and friends forever.
Sharing one cover this summer.

Restricted Performance

Pulse drops so low.
No sign of a heart beat.
Eyes turn over in disbelief
Safety is in question
Emergency is miles away
Fun looks like a solid blue grey
Ice is far beyond reach.
I can no longer feel my feet
Yet my safety blanket is providing
Heat. Not your time yet.
Dig deep and find a pulse, use it to
Base line a rhythm. In far distance
Listen to your favorite poem.
Wake up, it's not your time yet.
Only a restricted performance gallery.
Learn to offset and reset.

Main Mechanic

Pacemaker blues
Not sure who to call
Or what to do. Doctor is
On vacation with his family too.
My heart is beating like a drum
Now where is my shoe.
Call on the only one who can truly
Recharge your heart. Pray in silence
He's your emergency captain.
No charge is the price from your heavenly
Mechanic. Your lifeline to restart your
Engine. Only one loose cross wire.

Provision

Provide for your people oh Lord
Prepare us for eternity.
Shelter us from any unknown source
Keep us safe from iniquity.
Forever we will need your forgiveness
And continuous love.
Uplift every thoughts travelling on this
Journey. Be our source oh Lord.

What Is Our Purpose

Love one another to the core
Be there for each other
Forever more.
Share your gifts, share your burdens
Stand in the middle of nowhere.
Find your purpose then act on it.
Help along the wayside. Create a comfortable
Space. No good deed should be wasted.

Pacemaker Scare

This device might scare you to death.
Wake up my friend, your still here
This is not a death trip. Focus and get a
Grip. Yes this is a foreign object
Look beyond the origin. Enjoy every journey
Have no fear, when you get a pacemaker scare
Your faith stands firm, welcome my dear.
This is just a pacemaker Scare.

Build My Courage, Take Away Any Pain

Send me to a retreat where no one knows
My name. Comfort me when i cry tears of joy
Abide with me, stay by my side.
Be me a foundation of hope and courage
Provide a safe Base for me to live.
Wash away my sins, start a fresh. Give me wings.
Build me a safe haven to call home.
Rebuild my Courage take away my Pain.

The Eyes Of Mankind

The eyes of mankind, carries the truth
The eyes of mankind store up lies
The eyes is the window to our souls
Keep it pure and clean. Wear your glasses
Clean your lenses, make sure your vision is
Accurate. Someone life depends on it.
Do not accept bribe, it's a corruption.
Stay focus with your eye contact intact.
No false statement, not even for the president.
The eyes of mankind holds the Vision of Truth.

When Your Time Is Up

Make that call to heaven, tell your immediate
Family and friends that you're going home early
Feel free like a bird, ready to fly away.
Love will be the only energy needed, leave some behind
For everybody. What a beautiful feeling when we're
Finally rested. With our savior. Walking hands in hands
With the saints. Drink water from your favorite cup
When your time is up. So peaceful. This chapter.

Feeling Good Today

This is when your mind body and soul is on a balance scale
Feel your stress and any negative energy drift away.
Feel your burden gets lighter, your scale starts to show
Success and improvements.
Feel good today, all your bills are paid. Your goals are met
Safety is everywhere for you to see. Positive is a daily bread
Everyone is beautiful and ready to be a productive force.
Feeling good today is hard work. Nothing happen overnight.
Work harder, you will achieve your goal. Continue this trend
It's a continuous testament, only thing is this is my poem.
Smooth sailing.

Poetry From Behind The Scene

Read my poetry in every situation.
Read my poetry when you're in a wagon
Read my poetry on the train
Read my poetry when you're enjoying the rain
Read my poetry in every given challenge
Read my poetry before you enter the ring
Read my poetry when you did'nt study a thing
Read my poetry to boost your positive side
Read my poetry, i already plug you in.
Gifted from behind the scene.
So go ahead, read my poetry. It's fireworks.
It's Fireworks all the time.

Close To My Heart

Draw closer to me
Find the clue that control
My passion fruit.
Try to find me in moment of
Silence.
This is a start, some day you
Will get close to my heart.
One day your heart will find
Me, standing in paradise
Gather your broken pieces
Slowly we'll be whole again
Let's start out as friends.

Gone Way Too Soon

Far far away, in the midst of the
Ocean, i can see your beautiful face.
Far far away beyond the clouds
Your love and grace forever will be
Far beyond every avenue
I can smell your perfume coming from the tree
From beyond the stars, i can see your
Smiling face looking back at me.
My way of saying memories will forever be.
Good people, gone way too soon.

Pacemaker Blues

Prayer will be your friend to keep
Perseverance will be under the sheet
Your strength will be uplifted by your
Faith. Deep in your thoughts will be a
Carriage of love to take.
Wisdom is close by, research you maintenance
Kit. Learn as much about safety within.
Leave every energy to the Lord.
He knows best. Pass this test.
Lets go for a walk to crush this pacemaker
Blues. Carry all your positive tools.

Shine In Your Glory

Shine in every room
Never a dull moment
Love openly to allow the
Blood flow to carry on.
Travel with a peace of mind.
Give so much, never out give yourself.
Feel free to explore your happiness
Live your life to the fullest.
Shine in your glory.
Use me for a bed rest.
Only the strong will live to tell
Read and express yourself.
Ring the humanity bell.
Always shine in your glory.

Before I Go To Sleep

Clean my slate oh Lord
Hand me down a pure heart
Forgive me of all my sins
Allow only good within.
Embrace my way of life
Uplift others in their livings
Cleanse my soul before i go
To sleep.
Be my guardian angel.
Without you, i would be nothing.
Search my heart and give me peace
Before i go to sleep.

My Last Breath

Life was filled with challenges
Vegetables and oranges
Lime juice and lemon with sweet
Grapes blended in.
Whatever the flavor in life we find
Our best fit and live in it.
Work hard with whatever to uplift.
A clean heart, with only love as lining
True family and friends just a phone call
Away. Peace be with you.
Resting in God's grace when i take my last
Breath. Heaven welcome me home. Angels
Awaits.

My Soul Mate

My heart open wide shut
The moment i met you
My ears was as clear as a
Whistle.
My eyes sparkles with a smile
Larger than life.
My body collapse in the midst of
Your presence.
I could feel the era of a new
Beginning. True feelings the day
I met my soul mate.
Never a dull moment. I can now sleep
With both eyes closed.
Finally at peace, with you watching over
Me. Cover me with your forever love.
My heart will do the same.
For my soul mate.

Sunshine Heart

Watching the sunrise in the morning
Embracing the sunset at night
Living for the moment with nature by
My side. Breathing in fresh air
Freedom to live my life
Caption of happiness walking with me
Enjoying the ocean breeze.
What would i do, if sunshine was'nt apart
Of this avenue.
Leave a room for the sun to shine in your
Heart,

Celebrity News

A celebrity died today
A very famous one
What ever the story is
This memory will live on
Forever.
The heart never forget the
One's who sacrifice their life
To help others.
When the birds fly, think of them
When it rains think of them
When the sunshine, think of them
When you love more than enough
Think of them.
Forever peace will follow all
Celebrity news.
Good Memories forever.

I Love The Rainbow

My heart now live for the moment
Every minute counts.
The beats are slower than before
My knees almost buckle to the floor
The rain drop bouncing off the window
Sill. When i open my eyes again for a new
Flow, in the distance i could see a beautiful
Rainbow. Calling me home is my Savior
Waiting patiently in the wings.
Come home my dear, i know that you love the
Rainbow. It will guide you home.
Safely to me..

Another Plane Crash

I feel like i am having an heart attack
Another plane crash.
Everyone is alarmed by this news
Every heart feels the pain
In the distance is my only memory of what
Could have happen.
Pray within the storm, we're family
Be there one for another.
This is a news flash
Another plane crash.
Take a deep breath, no need for another
Heart attack. Deep in the ocean, clues
Awaits. Let's pray for this shock to go away.

Apple Of My Eye

The son that knows my heart
The son that knows my love
Forever bonded with the apple
Of my eyes.
To the nation, watch over our
Children give them love, always
Feed them with the positive side of
Humanity. Teach them to share
A daughter now live to tell
The mother that knows her well.
Forever bonded with the apple
Of your eyes.

Missing You

I feel like a fish out of water
Without you.
My pillar is soaked with tears
Missing you just creep through
My brain sending the rough waves.
My body is weak with sweat running
Down my spine. Anxiety is my separation
Avenue. Missing you is now my nightmare
Dreaming is about to take me out
Call someday with a love poem
Send me place to have a heart beat again
Mail me a love note.
Capture my rhythm in this blue space
Teach me how to survive when i am missing you.

Pray For Every Child

The young minds
The innocent souls
The pure hearts
They're like gold
Shelter them with true
Love. Provide education on
Every door. Pray for every
Child to be on a safe avenue.
When there's a sickness
Help with the cure.
Peace will always travel with
Our children. Show them love.
Let us pray for every child.

The Nation Poet

The nation poet knows right from wrong
The nation poet will not see color
The nation poet will not see walls or borders
The nation poet will always have an open mind
The nation poet prays and meditate everyday
The nation poets provides love freely from the
Heart. Everyone could be the nation poet.
Open your heart to the universe allow humanity
Love to move in. Ask God to wash away all your sins.
Live daily to always be of help to others. Even if it's
A small chapter. Read and find peace within.
This is a note from the nation poet.
Pass it on.

Winning Is Easy

The group is ahead of the game
You'r'e still on your knees praying.
Your confidence level drops tremendously
Your memory is now a question sign
Your heart rhythm is calling your name
Focus on the most important factor the race.
The beginning of the journey is now yours
The final results is hanging over your head
Stay on par, stay in tune with your body chemistry
Drink your water no need for dehydration.
The group is falling back in their ideas
You're now ahead of the game.
Winning is your only focus.
Go ahead and win. Winning is easy.
You can own this poem.

Single Ladies

To all the single ladies
Never give up in life
Mr right is not mr right now
Focus on the main reason why
You want to be loved
Why is there a need to find someone
Use that thought to capture the hearts
Of others. Share and be open minded.
Love with a purpose. Mr right is doing
The same thing. You will run into each other.
Laugh when you read this gift, it was written
Specially for you. I was once a single lady too

Sunflower Spirit

Wake up my sleepy heads
The sun is coming out
The place is a mess
Check your hearts for
The charger.
Let's head out to the garden
To take a picture of the
Sunflower horizon.
It's facing the sun, it's swaying
In the wind. It has an emblem of
Our hearts, love shining through
This avenue.
Sunflower love to everybody
Share along every journey.
You're a sunflower too.

First True Love

The one that gives you butterfly
Mayday.
The one that sneak you out of the
House to watch the sunrise and the sunset.
The one with a genuine heart that
Flows directly into yours.
First true love that will never be forgotten.
Memories forever lives on. Beautiful melody
From the birds. Time well spent with your first
True love.

Look For Me

When your'e lonely, look for me
When you need a friend, look for me
When you feel like no one's child, look for me
Look for me in the midst of the ocean
Look for me to stand by you in your trials
Look for me to wipe your tear drops.
Look for me to share your joy and sorrows
My goal is to prepare you for tomorrow.
When in doubt, please look for me.
I will always be there, through the storm
Look for me, and always stay calm.
Pray and look for me.

Discover Your Heart

Your heart is a pump
It needs love to pump the blood flow
Hatred will delay this mechanism
Flourish your heart by helping others
Feed the poor, help, help the homeless
Heal the sick through poetry.
Pray for the nation, to only love one another
Discover your heart it's free to love all over
Again. Know your friends. Support your family
Expect nothing in return. Smile with everyone
Read this poem and discover your heart.

Author House

The number one self publishing company
Make no mistake, they would never turn
Their back on the poor man child. Every
Author is an open book, work hard and
Show what you got. Author house encourage
All with their positive vibes. Today i will uplift
This company on a pedestal. No special credit here
Just humanity love from a gifted soul.
Peace in paradise, let's eat as one family.
Abundance of Love for Author House

Usa In Bolt Legacy

Fast like an lightening
Showmanship to a tea
Sweet like a sugar
Jamaicans legacy supreme
Poor is never a crime
It's indeed a base to work from.
Struggles is a stepping stone
To uplift from within.
Never say never, promote the
Best. Usain bolt the legacy used
For this test.
A winner is always the one to challenge
Take this page and incorporate
Your own monetary value
Use it to uplift the nation. Legacy.
Forever bonded, the jamaican people.
Welcome USA in Bolt legacy

Promote Yourself

Use the gift God gave you
Promote yourself from every avenue
Search and you will find a comfort zone
Use your demeanor as a shelter street
Provide food for the needy
Send in the safety paradise for cool breeze.
Love spread on every table. Flowers for
Everyone who enters your world.
Suspense is mine to live.
Use the gifts that i gave you to promote
Yourself, be available to the chosen few
You're the only one on this avenue.
My words are clues.
Use it to promote yourself.

Heart Is A Gift

Your heart is a gift to mankind
Live to only see the good in people
Even when you are aware of the unknown
Open your heart to the universe
Only allow positive vibes to come in
Close when the negative blues try to take resident
Re-open to re-group and start over again.
Never forsake the homeless, never look down on
The weak. Never stop giving.
Your heart is a gift, i made you son.
Question not, just live to uplift all.

Poetry Pacemaker

Poetry pacemaker will go down in history
As the first one ever created.
It will be filled with lots of love for repair
Butterflies will be everywhere, surgical
Procedure will be manage closely by one
Universal precaution and sterilization will walk
Hands in hands. No need for a judgment zone
Everyone on board are prayer warriors
Line the heart with every powerful prayer
Use it to stop any pressure
Gauze along the way, safety will be in your thoughts
You will be your own mayday. Peace will follow your
Heart. Enjoy this poetry pacemaker. Someday you might
Find it very useful. I am with you always. Welcome your
New device. Poetry pacemaker.
A new beginning

Taking You There

Someday you will enter a suspense zone
Map out a structure in your mind
Use it for a guidance of some kind
Gather your knowledge for a baseline
Use your perseverance as solid gold
Find the path to success with the gifts
No man can take away from you.
Chosen is only given to a few
Taking you there is my chapter to finish.

Prodigal Son Come Home

Come to the family who already
Mourn their lost. Open your eyes
And breathe, you're still alive
Pick up the broken pieces, bond
Them together again.
Your life will feel like a wholegrain
Wash away your guilty feelings
Everything is forgiven
Prodigal one go home and count
The sand. Every number represents
Love at hand. Tell sadness to be gone.
You're a child of God.
Enjoy his blessings. We are one.
Prodigal child come home

Poetry For The Nation

We will be faced with life challenges
Use them to focus on the positive side
Of humanity. Remember safety your protective
Gear. Cover your heart, you will need it to
Map your way out of these challenges.
Your faith is your strongest mechanism
Do not fall along the way side.
Nature could be your first call
When your'e alone, find peace within.
Pray one for another, leave room to breathe
Search your soul, leave no room for error
Life is a challenge. Live it with a wellness in mind.
Always be very kind. Smile because life itself is always
A challenge.

Mentors Are A Gift From God

When you find time to help others
When you can feel others pain
When you offer your support
To give first and not to gain
When you feed the needy
When you share in every aspect of life
You're a mentor, continue on with your
Blessings. Special people cannot be used
Mentors are a gift from God.
Uplifting all mentors. Let's hold hands for
This energy to carry on to the next generation,

Be An Inspiration

Be an inspiration on a
Daily basis
Live to motivate.
Worry not
Forsake not
Compliment on every
Avenue
Cry tears of joy
Be happy even in your
Crisis.
Doubt not
Uplift your faith
Amazing grace. Only
Be an inspiration.
Be a helping hand.

Hospice Care

Be the anchor that pull in the ship
When you're weak, enter the room
With your deepest strength relief.
Swim along side the ocean for clue
No need to feel sorry for yourself
Ride the waves when you can be you.
Call on your best friend.
Hospice is never the end. In the distance
You will see the beginning of a new bend.
Comfort is your soul. Always focus on
We care. Hospice comfort care is everywhere.
Show love and empathy. Have no fear this is
Hospitality care.

God Is The Greatest

In times of need
Put all your trust in God
In time of despair, put all your
Hope in God.
In time of sickness devote all
Your energy towards God.
Every true messenger knows
That God is the greatest.
Get up off your doubt and
Reschedule your doctors
Appointment. Pray and be bless.
Our father God is the greatest.

Good Sportsmanship

Within the clavicle of our inner circle
Our ego will eat away our brain cells
Setting in high gear a sense of pride
In the same circle are the unique souls
They will say very little but observe a lot.
Calm yourself my dear, this is only a test.
The truth will show in the end.
The final result will require good sportsmanship.
Shake hands even with the enemy. Be brave.
A good Sportsman want to live and share

Enjoy congratulation and Criticism in the same box.

Speak To The Nation

The heart that speaks to the nation
Will be the heart that knows pain
The voice that can feel your motion
Will be the voice that already know
Your name.
The soul that is deeper than the ocean
Will be the soul bless to accommodate all.
Beyond our journey is the masters call
Answer with only love in your heart.
Share his blessings and speak to the nation.
This is a new start.
Speak to the Nation

Princeton University Hospital

Patient first was their scope of practice
Up to date in services was always a learning
Experience. Promote your best and uplift
Each other. We're one big family tree
Give back to the community, share our love
Around the world. This is the call to uplift
At princeton university hospital. Best in
Customer satisfaction.
Past employee, happy memories.
Forever bonded. A word from the gifted.

Sunlight Chapel

Peace in our time of rest
Peace spending time alone
Peace in our travels with God
Peace in that special moment
Peace with our faith family and
Friends. Peaceful is the heart that
Knows only love. Comfort knows your
Soul. Peace be with you all.
From the sunlight chapel of gold.
Peace, peace, peace.

The Poorest Child

The poorest child i sent to college
Will be the only one who remembers
My name, when i am long gone.
The poorest child with the richest soul
Forever we will be apart of history.
True love is an education
Pass it on like you are in a relay
Win the race to success. The poorest
Child experience the most challenge
Then they strive to be the best,.

Turn Over A New Leaf

This leaf is a very powerful leaf
Filled with lots of positive energy,
Use it to heal your soul.
It came from the tree of life
Everyone is the root.
The prayer that lives on will
Heal our souls forever.
It will be the best medicine.

In The Eyes Of The Ocean

In the eyes of the ocean
I can see your face.
At the bottom of nature
Your roots are maturely gray
Lining the heart with pure
Flowers, beautiful soul
Floating by.
In the eyes of the future
Everyone will know your name.
The dream of the gifted.
The light that will uplift your flame.
In the name of humanity true love
Lives deep within.
In the eyes of the ocean
I can't even swim.

Mobile Book Store

The word of the gifted
Will be a gift for the nation
The mobility will be close
At hand. Every church
Every center, every homeless
Shelters. Everyone with a
Voice will be given a chance to
Express themselves. No table will
Be empty. Everyone will be filled
With positive vibes to feed the nation.
Spread the gift of love for others to
Follow. Mobile book store.
First written in the form of poetry.
A true gift for eternity.

Bill Clinton Gone Too Soon.

In the eyes of the gifted
The soul wonders away
In the heart of mankind
The part that will never decay
The love that will stand every test
Of time. The pacemaker is a foreign
Visitor. Will only hold up for a time
As an object. The butterfly weeps.
Mankind stands still with their eyes
Wide open. Where is the mindset of
The future, if the presence predict it
First. The voice that will be the leader
Of the nation, will someday find peace
With the powerful source in poetry.
Rest in peace bill clinton.
A Dream wrapped up in a Prediction Suit.

Life Is A Peaceful Tree

Life is the root of our existence
It travels with us everywhere we
Go. It holds up in difficult times
It survives on the positive growth
Life is the oxygen we breathe
Keep it clean from all negative
Energy. Stay away from pollution that
Will corrupt your soul.
Love even when the storm is near.
Draw closer to the one that will always
Know your name.
Shalom! Life is a peaceful avenue
Plant your seed to success.
Give everyone this poem.
Take a moment for rest.

Creative Minds

When the creative mind
Can caption the notion of
Two images. The judgement
Zone of the curious will rise
Tremendously.
Focus and always walk with a
Goal in mind. Explore and spread
Your safety net.
Creative minds are the geniuses of
The future.Today is yours. Spend it
Wisely. Seek out the creative minds
Around you. I will be the judge
You will seek the school.
Searching for the creativity in you.
Enter with an open mind.
Five minutes to write me a creative poem.
This is a forum for a new crew.

Extraordinary Life

I do not live in a ordinary world
I live in a extraordinary life.
Same avenue just taking a different
Approach. Two successors just
Travelling into different paradise.
Extraordinary life extraordinary
Root springing from that tree.
Extraordinary life foundation is
Run for everybody. Poetry gravy
For the needy. Uplift with a special
Degree, everyone is family on my
Family tree. Extraordinary life is
To love and welcome anniversaries.
Remember birthdays and special occasions
Passions go along way. Life is a free spirit
Extraordinary me.

Midst Of The Storm

In the midst of the storm
The curious minds will still wonder
To find the passions of life.
In the midst of the storm the doubters
Will lost their momentum in order to
Find their shelter. In the midst of the
Storm the givers will continue giving
The takers will continue taking.
Every purpose will be different.
Accommodate the open minds, call them
To comfort the creative ones. The humble
Souls will pray. Peace will be your rest in the
Midst of the storm. Be calm.

Sunshine Heart

The heart with sunshine bouncing
Off every chamber, will be the
Heart strong enough to sparks mine.
The heart with the glaze of happiness
Coming from the aorta will be strong
Enough to welcome my smiles.
The sunshine heart will be my smiley face
In difficult times. My best friend will be
My saving grace. Deep within the pump is
Slowing down. Enjoy life this is a poetry
Pacemaker. Compliment every test, it's a
Guessing factor. Everyone heart is lined with
Love. Sunshine flowing from within the beats.

Focus On Humanity

Focus on the good in people
Focus on the rain and their pain
Focus in the midst of pressure
Help to go around the border
Focus in their most difficult
Challenge. Your gift is to be of
Good tidings.
Stay focus on humanity.
My job is to help you through.
Rest on the positive avenue
For good news. Spread love to every
Soul. Borderline the heart too.
Balance and find comfort beside you.

My Heart Is Open

Open your heart to me my dear
My heart is open to you without fear
The energy needed is a
Shock from two powerful souls
The rhythm of my heart will heal
Your pain. The beat from your pump
Will raise my pressure to carry on.
This is a moment to gain.
Within the wall of mercy. You will find
Me. Our hearts will learn to beat again.
Baby steps all over for fun. Send us the rain
With blessing from this strain. Happy to be
Home again. Amen

Road To Success

Walk with me on this road to success
We travel along way by train
Some walk the long journey just to
Say my name and press replay again.
Hold my hands in the rain. Smile with
Our progress, send me a note for
Encouragement. Teach me to love beyond
My last breath. We can still take a step to
Success. Every stage is worth fighting for
This is a new beginning, others are facing the
End. Road to success is just around the bend
Go deep in your bravery machine, pull out your
Perseverance, use it for a sheen.
On every road,there's a stop sign. Follow direction
You're in the road to success. Welcome.

Dance And Sing

Dance and sing add poetry to find the rhythm
Embrace life all over again. Mri is not boring
It's a test for music and poem to glide in.
Fix the mind of the one with the heart of steel
Dance to the poem that will reveal a new meal
A new inventory that will welcome your heart
Beats in the tune of a poem. Plug in the answer
Before the question. Drive home the most powerful
Sound of your heart ring. Dance and learn to pace
Beats from the main pump. Waves into rhythm sent.
Release every pressure and be brave.
Lets dance and sing, all over again.

Michael Jackson Chosen Angel

The child that lives in us
Cries out loud,to face our adulthood.
Our secret pain is stronger than success
Itself. The sunshine is a safe haven to wrap
Around natures paradise.
The reality of our souls expands in circle
Our cage is a unique paradise. Safety lives
Close by. Home is the heart of the child that
Lives in us. Innocent is the method used to mend
The broken heart. Our loyal friends are family
Forevermore we will once again face the truth.
Michael jackson a glimpse of my chosen angel.

News For The Nation

Something went wrong again
Something very alarming
My friends.
Everyone mouth is wide open
With shock and denial rhythm
Violence and evil touch base
We started to feel like there's
No love in this place.
News, everyone will seek a safety
Net, the enviroment is polluted and
Is creating a mess.
No one is safe in a open space
Focus on your family and close your
Gate. Run for cover a new president
Is taking over the border. Caos over
The minds that you believe don't matter
News, keep in mind, everyone could be
Sisters and brothers. Peace hug to you

Labor In Your Day.

It's another day. Fun lurks into our
Minds. Others find a way to unwind
Far in the distance a loud explosion
Out of nowhere, will spoil all the fun.
Labor day, a beautiful day for things to
Turn around. Find safety first then help
Your fellow men comprehend.
On labor day, the only medicine needed is
For everyone to pray away.
Call for peace on labor day.
No one should perish this way.

Marketing Challenge

Writing for every energy
Marketing monkey
Bush baby, everyone is
A moment from controversy
The words fits human in our
Loyal friends world. Yet this
Frame could hold someone else
Use your imagination in this moment
To complete a project. The creative
Mind, will take over the world of
Marketing someday. Pace yourself and
Be your best on the chart. Now give me
A view of your work of art.

Balance Your Life

Balance life with a grain of salt
Apply sugar to spice things up.
Adopt to the energies that drives us
Adjust to change, embrace life today
Let the sunshine reveal your tomorrow
Love the nation with open arms
No one travels on a perfect avenue
Seek peace within, this is a beautiful way
To balance your heart, give me your hand
My heart need a boost too. Mold this for two.

Jesus Money

If Jesus was on earth today
He would be the same way my dear
His goal was always to help
The poor, uplift the rich in their endeavors
So why should i think differently. This is
Jesus money, give some away to the poor
Let it rain on the needy on their blue day
Bright up the world with the rainbow
Send everyone out to play. Flow your kisses
Around, this could be a merry go bound
This is Jesus money, attach it to my poem and
Give it a way. View me in the distance waving.
Good my dear, it's Jesus money, we have to share
And give some away. Still leave some for mr rainy
Day.

Everyone Will Move On

Everyone will move on someday
Pray and ask God for forgiveness
Then open the heavens gate.On replay
Welcome faith, friends and your families
Do not look too far for me.
My place is at Jesus feet, thanking him
For all his earthly challenges, a quiz
Everyone will be a angel someday
Save a place in your heart for me
I want to be your play date on the other side
Just remove a pacemaker and re-cycle me
Butterfly your way home. Hospice, no more pain
Everyone will move on someday. Embrace the rain.

Thread The Needle

Go ahead and thread the needle
Remember to leave room for a lea way
Do not shake hands, prevent the spread
Of infection. Sterilize the heart with love
Baseline with prayer, copy the zest for life
Spread your wings, i am with you always.
Meditate before they apply anesthesia.
Think beautiful angel. Thread the needle, i will
Hold your hands forever.

Universal Precaution

Everyone is treated in the same light
Safety is a thread mill.
Never loose your mindset
Patient first.
Practice what you preach
Make your words bonded.
Gather everything beautiful
Make a rainbow for you and i
Long life, to live all over again.
Remember me at the universal
Precaution line. Be on time so we
Can unwind.

Poetry Soup Dish

Washing our hands is a must
Gather all your ingredients
All your seasoning and your
Cultural surprises for cure
Keep your meat as a secret
Mine will be on broadcasting
Chicken foot soup from way
Yonder, best known in jamaica.
Dispose of the toes, cook it until
It melts, share with all your family
And friends. Now tell me your secret
I can smell fish head soup, no problem
Man, that was going to be my first choice
Get the work shop ready for poetry stew.
It's all about creative minds, enjoy my
Poetry soup dish. Welcome to invite the nation
To the next one. Your dish taste the best.

Exotic Jaguar

Take your breath away
Find the opening to every center
Search the passions of life in your
Area. Live your life to the fullest
Love to the core of every endeavors
V8 your way to the top, drive and drink
To a healthy living. Remember our loyal
Friends. Feel free to incorporate them.
Exotic jaguar this is your frame
Turn it into your own poem.
Expand your horizon.

I Wanna Be Like Jesus,

To show only love and humanity
Give until you remove un-surety
Share in the moment of silence
Be that shoulder to lean on
You're stronger than your doubters
Be a given gift to mankind.
Never doubt yourself in forgiveness.
Pray on and see us together
Someday, some sweet day we should aim
To be like Jesus.

Pace Yourself

Relax in the most difficult time
Retract your steps, search for a comfort
Zone. Arrange your battlefield to be calm
This is not a hurricane, it's not a storm
It's the doing of humanity justice
Remove yourself from any controversy
The tide is a wave that surrender in the midst
Of their trials and tribulations.
Cast not judgement, love across the table.
Your gift is for the nation, not to serve one man.
Forgive when in doubt, breathe and let me care for
Your pulse. Your heart is stronger than you think.
I monitor it daily with my prayers. Pace yourself
Find peace with your circle of friends.

Change The World

Change the world using your method
Poetry, ring in the safety net to humanity
Scope the kindness that lives within.
Capture the hearts of many
Leave room to spend quality time with one.
Change the world with the drive to carry on
When in sorrows i will hold your hands
When in pain, apply prayer prn
Universal is the heart that can see your soul
This is yet to be told, you can change the world.

Faith Is Free

Apply within, work is available
The only thing needed is your
Ability to see your need.
Find a space for everything
Gather all the broken pieces
Make them whole again.
Shed some honey for a sweet taste
Make the drink amazing grace
Love with the rest of the world
Your heart is your gold.
Diamond is a part of your soul.
Smile in the mind that never gets old.
Faith is free for everybody.
Apply with a scripted spirit and a
Story to share with me. Feel free.

Be Brave

Be brave, my service men
Be bold to the end
Be calm this is the most difficult
Battle yet.
Collect all your tools to stop
Controversy from feds.
Global is your mindset.
Think for everyone on board
Bold and brave is yours to keep
Prayers are with you from every
Angle. Mine is a triangle for a
Broadband. Someday we will shake
Hands.Safety first is my version.
Universal precaution is a way to play
With. Be calm, this poem is your first test.

Butterfly Technique

Repairing the walls and every corner
Of the heart. Seal the leaky valves
Clamp down on your fears, Jesus is always
There. Surround yourself with positive
Energy, your true friends and family
Stay away from infectious base
Sterilize in a circular motion
Leave all worries to doctor love
Dream of the one far and way beyond
Everything is possible.
Survival is a dream come through.
This a your comfort zone to heal peacefully.
From a butterfly technique.

Protect The Gifted

Shelter the one with the unique ideas
That's the one that will be strong enough
To feed the nation cover the mindset of the
Doubters, the gifted cannot feel their pain.
Save for the future, don't spend it all today
The gifted knows the way.
Success can be seen from miles away. Ride the train
Prevent yourself from being swept away.
Walk the path to a new anniversary.
Find a new way to be a helping hand to more people
Be the one soul who will protect the gifted.
Use their ideas to motivate others, never loose site
Of your dreams to give back.

Success Avenue

Set yourself up for success
Pass it down the line with
Flying colors. Everyone is here
For a reason. Now use your reason
To incorporate everybody.
Everyone is a poetry opening to
The page of their own story.
Success avenue will be named after
You. The natures child with the mind of
An angel. To see her, you have to be given
A gift to see me. Scrutiny was your first
Thought, drop it, let go of it. Now review
That line again. Success avenue is not just
For your friends. It's a walk for everyone
Who is recovering from a challenge.

Mentors Dream

The smartest one ever lived
Could be the one who teaches you almost
Everything. Maybe he or she was the only
One that could see something special in you.
They open the door and allow the gifted through.
Smile for the world to see. The mentors that give
And expected nothing in return, has a heart made
Of goals. The harder they come, you wont fall.
This is a reality, that was your mentors dream.
Work and help to bring the gifts out of you.
Every pores wide open to receive love.

My Prediction

Chaos everywhere, everyone is frustrated
Helpless and combative at the same time.
Law enforcement are at large, but they cannot
Do anything. The leaders safety net can only
Accommodate the rich. The poor man is out wide
Open to fend for themselves. The air is polluted
With something contagious floating around.
Universal precaution is practice by the very few.
Codes are thrown around like a grain of salt
Money means nothing to nobody. Love is everywhere.
Yet it will not be clear for everyone to see.
The end will be yours to keep. Hold on to a tree, this is
Just my prediction poetry. Without you there will be no me.

My Umbrella

I have room for two
My umbrella is wide open to welcome you.
Fit right under this shed my dear
The rain will stop very soon, my journey is far
From over, i can only assume that you're on
A journey too.
Whatever you do, find room to always helps
Someone else. My destination is here, but i am
Going to leave this umbrella with you. Continue on
With this gift. Welcome this poem as a clue
My umbrella will carry on and now work for you.

A Simple Sentence

Know the lines that will uplift your soul
Read the same line until you're fulfilled
Pass that energy around the room
Your goal is to find peace in the spur of a
Moment. Write down a sentence and pass it
Around. My line is simple. I love you for showing
Up we already have a purpose, we're here for
A reason, no one will feel left out, something
Will be a surprise. A simple sentence could go along
Way. Make it take your breath away. Say hurrah.

Write Your Name

Your name is already written
Spread the positive seeds around
Watch it grow into something beautiful
No one will carry their burden alone anymore
Everyone will chip in to help from within.
Write your name, Jesus already see your needs
Feel at rest, clothes food and shelter will be
Given to you short term until you're able to get
On your feet again. Here's a coupon, here's the number
Of a shelter. We're one body in this fight together.
Struggle no more my sisters and brothers, this is not
A game. Just go ahead and write down your name.

Beautiful Butterfly

Close your eyes and vision a beautiful butterfly
Open your eyes and see me.
Stand in that space and vision all over again
Now i see you in that same light.
Beautiful is all around in this room.
Oh what a delight to share.
Open your heart and imagine the birthday girl
Open your eyes maybe it's for a birthday boy
Smile make everything fun. When you think of
The butterfly. Your passion is alive and well
Fun land and a beautiful day to you, and you and you.

Sorry For Your Lost

You lost your husband
You lost your wife
You lost a very close family member
You lost your best friend this year
Everything happen for a reason
Pray and hold hands this season.
Never forget the good times you share.
Smile all over again, welcome new people
In. Your heart will heal again. It will take
Time to unwind. Function at your own pace.
This is at no cost. Sorry again for your lost.

Sunshine Dress

I will twirl for you in my sunshine dress
I feel so pretty with my new hair do.
I will dance until my dream comes through
This happy moment i would love to spend with you
Sparkles coming from my eyes, diamonds floating
Around the room, i feel dizzy just thinking about a clue
This must be the love that goes with my new shoe
Glitters and fairy tales with disney blue.
Sunshine dress will do this to you too. Shock this
Moment and draw a review. Sunshine dress, think outside
The box, now be you, a creative fox.

Bring Out The Models

Johnny long legs
Bring out the models.
Walk the run way be yourself.
Confidence is everywhere in sight
Men and women feeling alright.
Stars and geniuses work of art on
Display. One poet with this written poem
Music with fun rhythm. Dancing hearts
Everywhere changing for the next show.
Zoom in closer, and bring out the models.
Paparazzi will steal the show,someday
The table will be turn, make them the guest
For a replay test. Bring out the models again.

Hold Me Close

Hold me close, cry me to sleep
Comfort my soul without the sheet
Whisper my pain away, send me a treat
Safe my dignity, whatever i have left.
Reserve my time with you the best.
Hold me close and cry me to sleep.
Precious moments my blend to retreat
Forever we will be close for keeps.
Preserve our love for the next week.
Just hold me close. And rock me to sleep.

Marketing Genius

Demonstrate that one thing in abundance
Apply your skills and your special eye.
Be different to the bone.
Everyone is not the same. Ideas floats away to
Start a new stream somewhere else.
Marketing could be a toy, created by a little boy
The genius with the biggest idea, could be a little
Girl. Find a comfort zone and enter this same avenue
Over and over again. Practice what you preach and
Spread in the world of marketing. Nothing for nothing
Is nothing. Give everyone this poem. They will get the
Message about marketing.

Social Media

Expand your horizon
Social media can make you or break you
Focus on your dreams.
Everyone is looking for something
Do not leave yourself out of nothing
Social media is cut a throat
Leave yourself secure, do not leave much
Room to be at a lost.
Gain momentum when they recognize that you're
The genius poet that could work for everybody
Gravy. Social media make it work for you too
Your mother didn't raise no jamaican fool.
Social media is for followers. Look at the
Abundance on twitter, chip in and followback
Mutual respect to all your facebook friends.
Social media exposure all over again. I am not
Surprise it took you this long to order a book.
My success to you.

Under The Dark Clouds

Moving across the skies
The sight of dark clouds
It's going to rain, but it will
Not be the same. Thunder and
Lightening seems like a big scare
Sitting at my window with eyes
Wide open. The birds are posing from
The palm tree in the distance.
Under the dark clouds will be a poem from
The gifted, meditate on the positive and
Make it rain showers of blessings everywhere.
The storm is near, your job is to have no fear.
After the showers, welcome a beautiful rainbow.

Never Loose Hope

Believe in your dreams
Never loose hope in anything
Practice to believe in your
Faith. Hope is an open gate.
Be healthy and help the sick
Be strong and help the weak.
Believe in your dreams
You're chosen to do acts of kindness
Learn to bless and be blessed.
Give without mercy your Jesus baby.
Forever loved by everybody.
Be a gift to everyone you meet and greet
No one will forget your presence.
Keepsake is you.

Be That Change

Be the change no one saw coming
Think only positive, help everyone to
Live on a daily bread.
See yourself as the change that will
Uplift the world, love the light of day
Learn to love in the darkest moment.
Guide others into the light. Follow your
Dreams. Be that change that no one saw coming
Root out the good in everyone then plant a tree
Watch it grow into happiness. Be that change.

My Gift

My challenge was'nt easy
My gift was created for me
My heart was always at peace
My soul has a way of shielding
The weight from the start.
My mind is not yours to own
My skills will be shared evenly
My love is an open book.
Winning is in my genes
Copy that line and apply it to your
Dream too. My gifts will someday be
Very clear for you to view. Now this
Poem is not for your dog to chew. Here,
Purchase a new dress and learn to appreciate
Others success. My challenge will be your
Test.

Satan Hates Me

I am not love by one
I have no intention to feel
Sorry for myself.
Satan doesn't means me well
His plan for me is corrupted and
Filled with lies. Restless will be
My night if i allow him in my sight
Depart from me satan, you will never
Be my friend. Jesus already provided
For me. Without him i would think that
No one loves me. Sorry satan i am taken
By the creator of us all. A wider horizon
To love everyone, even when we fall.
Satan continue to hate me, because i only
Have eyes for God.

Soul Sisters

Two sisters born dirt poor
Neglected by a earthly fathers love
We watch mother struggles in her lonely
Pain. We hope the rain would wash her
Sorrows again. Two sisters now authors.
When neglect was giving out, two sisters
Knows everything. Yet silence creeps to
Protect the neglect from a family tree.
Soul sisters will always find love within
The hearts of childhood memories.
Poetry is a root to grow into something
Beautiful. Never depend on your family tree
To judge who you are. Especially if your family
Did not acknowledge your presence. Give God
All the praise. He will rebuilt the family tree.
Soul sisters peace.

Humble Child

A humble child will observe a lot
A peaceful soul maybe, you're not.
A humble child will stay still and calm
Praying internally for a peaceful ending
To every situation.
A humble child is now a gifted soul.
Protect the open heart that's lined with
Gold. Find your open mind for this chart.
A humble child is in this room, today you
Will welcome this avenue. Grow up and be
A humble adult too. Stay calm in the storm.
You are always loved by one.

All Grow Up Now

All grown up now
Ready to see whats out there.
I feel like a bird leaving the nest
All grown up, now it's time for me
To find a job in the entertainment
Business, where is a unique spot for me.
After all i want to be a walking poet's tree
Jamerican poetry could work at sea.
All grown up, standing in an open space to
Fulfill my basement with no more degree.
The gifted will be a prodigy. Please don't be
Overwhelmed, success will grow on every tree.
All grown up now, hats off to everyone in this
Room. Everyone survive our bird nest.
Enjoy change.

Find True Love

True love will find you
Hunt you down and take
You captive. Make sure
That's what you want.
False love will find you
Then try to impress you
Know the difference.
Know your needs,separate
From your wants. Search for
Your deepest passion, now
Find true love and pamper your
Heart.

Love The Haters

It's going to be hard,just try to
Love the haters.
Love their false pretense
Just don't apply it to your
Existence. Learn to love them
Through their trials.
They will soon see that your love
Is walking on a string.
Love the haters because our heavenly
Can see their heart too.
Forgive when you can. Your love will
Be strong enough to see you through.
Love, love, love even the haters in your
Prayers.

The Gay Life

You will face challenges
You will be ask to check your
Pulses. Face the music and feel free.
Jesus loves everybody. Search your
Soul and make him your best friend.
He will watch over your safety to the end.
People will always pass judgement.
Enjoy your faith and be open minded.
Love to all gays, my poems will never judge.
Pure love in the form of a rainbow to you.
Jesus will see you through any challenge.
Pray in silence and find peace within.

Mother To The World

A mother's love is like a garden filled with flowers
Every child deserves a mothers love to embrace
A mothers love is like abundance of hope and grace
Everything will be a challenge, a mothers love makes
It much easier. Giving and sharing from the heart will
Help to nourish the gift of a mothers love.
Be a mother to the world. And safe the children for the
Future.They need your light to follow.

Sunflower Baby Queen

Sunflower baby, bright up my night
Read me a poem for a good night delight
Sunflower baby beautiful to see
Parents around the globe will celebrate
With me.
Yellow green and bold will be your creativity
Sunflower baby lives in every home.
Safety visits with all my poems.
Sunflower baby, everyone will learn how to read.
Then earn them over again on christmas day.
Share a sunflower baby today.

Super Bowl

Super bowl
It's here again
Super bowl and
The millions of
Fans. You will be
The high expectation
You could be the most
Valuable player.
So much at stakes.
Your dream is hanging
By a thread, two teams
Left, may the best man wins
The winners will own this
Poem. Gifted for the world to
Read. Final score will be close
In prediction. 32-24 Cheers to
The winner in you.
Super bowl football galore.
Have fun when you read my score.
Show it door to door. My gift to you.

Make It Your Own

You can follow me on twitter
You can friend me on facebook
You can throw me hook as long
As it took.
You can only be invested when you
Own one of my books.
Read all my poems in cyber world
Make it your happy bird.Then twirl.
The truth of the matter is
If you could never own my book then
It might take you as long as it took.
To make it your own. Make sense the
Moment you order a gifted book.

Mankind Have Failed

Grace every moment, when you see the
Sun moon and stars. When in question about
Your nature side. Be not afraid to say that
Mankind have failed.
Mankind has failed in the loving dept
Mankind has failed to help their own
Mankind have failed at the highest level possible
Show increase love for nature, welcome the birds
And the trees, when ask why, simply say out loud.
Mankind have failed.
Failed tremendously.
Now let me enjoy the sunshine, then welcome the rain.
Blessing to you. Even though mankind has <u>failed us</u> long
Time ago. This is the time to let go, and help others
Who mankind have failed critically.

First Woman President

The first woman president will be someone who is strong
Enough to follow their dreams.
Focus enough to give all credit to God
Bold enough to write out her dreams for the public to read
The first woman president knows, what it means to grow up
Poor. The loop hole that will be created for the first woman
President in the usa, will be monitored by one.
Safety can only be practice accurately by the one who thread
It closely to their faith. May God continue to bless America.

I Appreciate You

I appreciate you for showing up
I appreciate the fact that you
Brought some family and friends.
I appreciate your kindness
I appreciate this moment.
The most important fact for this
Poem, is my appreciation, and it
Involves you.
I appreciate we do.

Jamaican Legacy

Thanks for welcoming me to your
Country. Thanks for sharing your
Culture with me.
From this day forward, everyone will
Be free to enjoy a piece of jamaican legacy.
My poetry is a work of art for everybody.
Feel this moment,when you need a friend
Think of me. You're not the only one.
Comforting thoughts, jamaican legacy.
Blue mountain.

BE GRATEFUL

BE GRATEFUL FOR EVERYTHING
EVEN IF IT'S A SIMPLE POPCORN RING
SHOW RESPECT TO EVERYONE
WE'RE HERE TO BE HAPPY
BE GRATEFUL, RARELY FEEL SORRY FOR
THE PRESENCE OF YOUR ENEMY.
WELCOME THEM WITH AN OPEN SPACE
SHARE THIS MOMENT, WITH THE BASE
NO ONE IS PERFECT.
IN EVERYTHING SHOW GRACE AND BE
GRATEFUL..

THE GIFTED SOULS

WHEN YOUR'E GIFTED, STAY IN THAT CIRCLE
NEVER TRY TO FIT IN. THE CHAOS OF TRYING
TO PLEASE EVERYONE WILL BE YOUR THUNDER BALL
STAY FOCUS AND BE CAREFUL NOT
TO TRIP OVER YOURSELF
EVERYONE WILL BE SYMPATHETIC,
YET STILL WILL BREAK OUT
LAUGHING. GIFTED ARE NO FOOLS,
JUST UNIQUE CREATIVE SOULS.
THEY HAVE ENOUGH GIFTS TO GO
AROUND THE WORLD, WITH YOU.

REACH OUT

REACH OUT AND TOUCH SOMEONE TODAY
THIS IS THEIR MOST CHALLENGING MOMENT
FOREVER SHOW LOVE, EVEN WHEN OTHERS
RUN THEM AWAY TO FEEL ABSENT.
REACH OUT AND GIVE A HELPING HAND
MY BLESSINGS TO YOU, WILL BE IN THIS POEM
REACH OUT AND BLESS SOMEONE TODAY
PASS IT AROUND. MY FRIEND. ONE FAMILY UNIT
IS THIS REACH OUT GAME. I WANT TO PLAY TOO.
REACH OUT AND TOUCH THEN PRESS REPLAY
PRAY ALL OVER AGAIN, REACH OUT THIS WAY.
THIS ROOM IS NOW A BRIGHT AND SUNNY DAY.

HEART THAT LOVES

OPEN YOUR HEART TO THE UNIVERSE
ALLOW THE OPEN SPACE TO BE FILLED WITH LOVE
SUSPENSE WILL BE EATING YOUR SOUL AWAY
IT'S OKAY, STILL LEARN TO OPEN
YOUR HEART ANYWAY.
WELCOME ALL BIRDS, LEAVE A EXTRA SPACE FOR THE
TURTLE DOVE. NATURE WRAP
AROUND WITH THE LOVE
FOR PEOPLE. SMILING ALWAYS, IS
THE HEART THAT ONLY
SHOWS LOVE.

LAST POEM

THIS IS THE LAST POEM
THIS IS NOT MY LAST BOOK
YOUR'E CHOSEN TO READ AT THIS MOMENT
IT'S A HOOK. OR A COOK BOOK.
A REQUEST FROM YOUR GUARDIAN ANGEL.
HE WANTS ME TO RING THIS GOLDEN BELL
SHE WANTS ME TO TURN THIS POEM INTO A SONG
FOREVER YOU WILL BE MY BABY. SING ALONG.
THIS IS MY LAST POEM, RING MY BELL. THEN READ
ME MY LAST POEM AGAIN.
FROM OUR GUARDIAN ANGELS. RESTING PEACEFULLY
IN HEAVEN. BONDING TOGETHER
ARE FAMILIES AND FRIENDS.
READING MY LAST POEM.

Printed in the United States
By Bookmasters